D1339134

Contents

Introduction   1

Volunteering?   6
Why Employ a Land Girl?   11
The Job   14
A Dangerous Occupation?   22
The Men   26
Board and Lodging   31
Social Life – Year One   35
Social Life – Years Two to Five   42
The Gangs   50
The Timber Corps   54
The Seasons   62
The War Experience   67
The Medal   73

Acknowledgements   77

Introduction

I was an academic member of an academic family in Leeds with my sights firmly set on Cambridge. So why did I spend some of 'the five best years of my life' as a farm labourer? And why in Scotland?

The attraction of Scotland was deep-rooted. Members of my mother's extended family were amongst hundreds of Scots who emigrated to Poland after the Napoleonic Wars. Hit by the economic depression which followed the Wars, they were recruited by Polish aristocrats to introduce advanced technologies in farming, engineering and textiles to their economically backward estates. Staunch Protestants, they rarely intermarried with Roman Catholic Poles. They retained their British passports and the successful often sent their children back to Scotland for school and university. My grandfather Thomas Garvie was sent to the Edinburgh Institution while it was still on Queen Street and had not yet become Melville College. His brother Alfred was one of the first day-boys at George Watson's College and his sisters went to the Merchant Maidens' School. Alfred then went on to Glasgow and Oxford Universities and became a distinguished theologian and principal of New College, London. Thomas returned to Poland and was the third generation of Garvies to become managers, directors, and finally partners in the Zyrardow factory which was reputed to produce the finest linen in Europe.

But ties with Scotland were never broken. Returning to Britain before World War I, my mother and her family were familiar with the vocabulary of Burns which her ancestors had taken out to Poland a century earlier. They were more Scottish than the Scots.

Part of my father's education had also been abroad. After the early death of my grandfather, a Dumbarton architect, his widow discovered that life in Switzerland was cheaper than in Scotland. From George Watson's College he was moved to Lausanne, where he remembered standing up for Britain in the playground of L'Ecole Cantonal during the Boer War. My parents met as students at Glasgow University but, after his graduation as a bacteriologist, work took them to England. My mother made sure that their seven children should grow up as Scots; my father that they should be hardy.

Our home was within ten minutes walk of my father's laboratory at Leeds University. In the centre of town, there was no 'nice' primary school within the walking distance of five-year-olds, so my mother taught us till we were nine and made sure that Scottishness was well and truly drummed into us. We all learnt about William Wallace and Robert the Bruce and the spider. After repeated defeats in his attempts to drive the English out of Scotland and seize the crown, Bruce was deeply demoralised. Hoping to escape to Ireland, he watched a spider trying to spin its web across the mouth of the cave in which he was hiding. When, on its third attempt, it succeeded, Bruce was inspired to return to the fray. Bannockburn followed and I knew that good Scots would never kill a spider.

Holidays in the Highlands probably made even more impact than our mother's history lessons. Spean Bridge, Newton Stewart and Dunvegan, the home our ancestors had left in the eighteenth century, were followed by Croft Cappanach, a house near Pitlochry which my parents rented every August. This became our second home. As Gaelic was still spoken in Perthshire in the mid-twentieth century, my mother could use the language she had studied at Glasgow University and on Sundays my father and my brother Tommy could wear their kilts. During the week daddy concentrated on turning us into respectably hardy Scots.

He had abandoned hope of toughening my mother. She could ride and dance - my father could do neither - but the boarding school for young ladies at which she had been educated in Warsaw did not have physical education on its curriculum. Her introduction to camping in Britain was a disaster: a week's rain in the Lake District followed by an even wetter week in Galloway terminated her career as a camper. With his children he was more successful, but Leeds was not a challenging environment. Use of the car was limited to taking the frail to church and the young were expected to walk everywhere, trying desperately to keep up with their elders. Most winters there was sledging, skating on frozen mill dams and, on Boxing Day, a hockey match on university playing fields, the teams a mixture of McLeods and medical students. The absence of a referee always upset Catriona, the only one of my sisters who was a born keeper of rules.

In the summer, on nearby university courts, there could be tennis before breakfast, but serious toughening was only possible during the Augusts at Croft Cappanach. Attempts to teach us to swim in the chilly waters of the River Tummel were less than successful but, on the hills, we made impressive progress. From Ben Vrackie's 2,757 feet we graduated to the more distant Ben Macdui's 4,300 – the second highest mountain in Britain. There was a memorable picnic on its snow-clad summit; Catriona and I shivering in our short skirts and knee length stockings while my father and a friend enjoyed their post–prandial cigarettes, snug in their tweed plus-fours. Riding breeches had been acceptable for women for many years and shorts were just coming in for serious tennis players, but it was after World War II before women were able to enjoy the comfort and freedom of trousers as everyday dress.

The culmination of the training programme was the classic walk from Blair Atholl to Braemar. This was mercifully shortened by my oldest sister Lilias who had just passed the recently introduced driving test. She drove us up the few miles of Glen Tilt accessible to cars and the following day picked us up in Braemar. But it was still a formidable walk, well over twenty miles. Inspired by John Buchan, my father (a responsible adult?) decided that we should sleep in the heather. This seemed a possibility until the rain came on, as did walking through the night until the path petered out in a bog. The toughening up must have been successful, however, because we all survived. To my father's efforts my brother had added boxing and my grandmother provided riding lessons. Every possible Saturday saw me at the stables where an hour spent mucking out stalls and cleaning tack earned me a free ride. By 1939 I was an exceptionally strong teenager. My father threatened that if he lost his job I could become the family earner as the strong woman in a circus. Fortunately, professors' chairs were secure.

Volunteering?

I was sixteen when World War II broke out. I had just passed the equivalent of a GCSE, which would have given me entry to other universities in Britain, but not to Oxford or Cambridge. Evacuated to a cottage in the Yorkshire Dales with my grandmother and two younger sisters, I settled down at Skipton High School for two more years at school and the possibility of an entry, if not a scholarship, to Cambridge. It was 1943 before conscription for women was introduced and it was easy to forget about the War.

My parents had been expecting a war ever since Hitler's unopposed seizure of the Rhineland in 1935. After Munich and Chamberlain's 'Peace with honour', my father started to dig an air-raid shelter in the garden. Disgusted by his lack of faith in the Prime Minister, a neighbour stopped speaking to him. In 1938 Germany had annexed Austria, in 1939 Czechoslovakia. Some of the many distinguished scientists, refugees from Nazi Germany for whom my father had helped to find work, became frequent guests in our home. The couple I remember most clearly were the Zinnemanns. In Nazi Germany the marriage of a Gentile to a Jew was illegal. Being Socialists, they had escaped to the USSR, where they were immediately imprisoned in separate prisons, suspected of spying for Germany. Neither knew that the other was alive until they were released a year later. I never knew how they reached Leeds but can remember the grey and shapeless woman who became beautiful when she recovered from the year's imprisonment in Russia. Nor have I forgotten the wonderful gingerbread houses she baked for us at Christmas. Her husband Kurt, a distinguished bacteriologist, was given a personal chair by Leeds University. We grew up knowing that Hitler had to be stopped.

A few weeks after Dunkirk I was concentrating on an essay on "The Causes of the Thirty Years' War" when my father arrived at the cottage. 'Mona,' he said, 'I must talk to you. I believe, as I always have done, on the importance of the higher education of women and, on the strength of your matriculation results, have obtained an Attestation of Fitness Certificate which will secure you a place to study history at the University of Edinburgh. But first we must concentrate on winning the war. I had arranged for you to work on the university farm near York but have discovered that it is surrounded by RAF camps. So perhaps it would not be a good idea. But Jessie' - the farm manager's wife and formerly my Girl Guide captain – 'has spoken to her father' - a dairy farmer in Galloway – 'and he could find work for you on his farm.' Two weeks later I had abandoned my essay on "The Causes of the Thirty Years War" and was on a train to Scotland, on my way to becoming a member of the Women's Land Army. It was many years later before the extraordinary nature of my 'volunteering' struck me. In the 1930s, decisions were made by parents and not by their teenage children.

As children my sisters loved dolls; I preferred miniature farm animals. Holidays at Croft Cappanach introduced me to a real farm where cows were milked and hay harvested so, unlike most Land Girls, I knew a little about farming. And the long walks and mountain climbing of our Highland holidays had indeed toughened me up.

About the Women's Land Army I knew absolutely nothing. It had been founded in 1917 when German U-boats had brought Britain to the brink of starvation. Fully industrialised, she had become dependent on imported food for both animals and people. By 1918, over 23,000 girls had been recruited and food rationing introduced: Britain had not starved.

In 1939, when Chamberlain's policy of appeasement had at last been abandoned, it was clear that a European war was imminent. Lady Denman, who had played an important part in its foundation in 1917, re-established the WLA in July. By September 1939, 1,000 girls had been trained and were ready to work; by December there were over 4,500 girls in employment, by 1943 over 80,000. I had not even seen a recruiting poster.

In England and Wales, with Lady Denman's home as its headquarters, it was a highly organised and independent organisation; in Scotland it was run by the Department of Agriculture in Edinburgh. In regions where there was a demand for Land Girls, either a 'county woman' or a member of a prominent farming family would be appointed to form the link between the Department, the local Farmers' Unions and the Girls. By 1943, when maximum numbers were reached, there were still very few Girls employed north of the Highland Line – six in Orkney and twenty one in Caithness. Ayrshire, a dairying county, was the only one in which there were over 1,000 Girls; in England over 1,000 was the norm.

In theory, volunteers were interviewed, medically examined, trained and sent to an appropriate job. I escaped all these formalities. But during my first month the farmer, Mr Armstrong, was paid by the government to train me and provide board and lodging. Board and lodging were excellent but training minimal. At the agricultural colleges at Auchincruive in Ayrshire, where most of the Glasgow volunteers were trained, and at Craibstone in Aberdeenshire, girls were introduced to cows, poultry, horses, tractors and agricultural machines and to market gardening and fieldwork. Many were then employed within commuting distance of Glasgow. My training was simpler. After a failed week with the cows, it consisted of making hay if the sun shone and cutting thistles when it rained. Perhaps the fact that the county representative, Mrs Grierson, who was Mr Armstrong's sister, had made me a special case. There seems to have been no supervision of the training provided by farmers or of the work done by representatives. They were all volunteers and unpaid. The Land Army was not disbanded till 1950, but some of the Girls recruited after 1945 received no training at all.

But I did get the uniform. Recruiting posters showed an attractive girl, in well-cut corduroy breeches and a green woollen sweater, making hay under a bright blue sky. The reality was rather different. The sweater was a pleasant colour and reasonably warm but the breeches could not have been more unbecomingly baggy. I wore my own riding breeches on formal occasions and, when working, hid the official ones under dungarees. The leather boots were never waterproof and the wellingtons sprang leaks months before we were entitled to the annual replacements. The belted raincoat was uncomfortable to work in, the hat flew off in a wind and, in winter, failed to protect our ears. In 1943 we got a short woollen coat. Designed by Worth, a well-known couturier, it was elegant – it hid the breeches – but inappropriate for heavy farm work. In the uniform provided for us to work in it was impossible to keep either warm or dry. In my first winter I had chilblains on my ears, hands, knees, heels and toes. It was not until I had acquired my brother's cast-off battle dress jacket and my grandmother's knee-length woollen knickers and bought myself waterproof leggings, gloves, a sou'wester and clogs that I discovered that it was possible to survive winter weather without acute discomfort. The clogs were wonderful. Lined with straw, cut to size and heated over the dairy boiler, they kept my feet warm and dry in even the worst weather. Having to return what was left of the official uniform at the end of the war was no hardship.

Why Employ a Land Girl?

Why would any farmer want to employ a Land Girl? Farming was a reserved occupation and neither farmers nor farm workers were called up. But many of the sons of successful farmers who had been sent to public schools and joined the OTC – the Officers Training Corps – volunteered. To grow the food which had previously been imported, extra labour was essential. Industrialisation and improvements in health and medical care in the late nineteenth century had increased Britain's population dramatically – Scotland's from 1,608,420 in 1801 to 4,760,904 in 1911. The population of the Highlands diminished but Glasgow's grew from 77,000 inhabitants in 1800 to over 1,000,000 in 1931. Britain was urbanised and the industrial revolution provided the wealth to pay for imported food. It had become cheaper to import food from abroad than to grow it at home. When war broke out German U-boats again made this impossible, but some lessons had been learnt from World War I. In the first few months food rationing was introduced and farming regulated. Marginal land cultivated during wars is not usually economically viable and, unless subsidised, reverts to rough grazing in times of peace. In 1939 this relatively unproductive land had to be brought back into cultivation. On a mixed farm a third of all the grassland had to be ploughed up and potatoes included in the crop rotation and all arable farming is labour intensive.

Until prisoners became available in the latter years of the war, women provided almost the only source for the extra labour needed. In the Lothians in the nineteenth century hinds, the married ploughmen, had to supply an unpaid female assistant at busy times of the year; women who had probably been working in the fields since they were children and had often become strong and skilled. They were known as the bondagers. Their work was seen by the farmers as payment for tied cottages. Unmarried women were often employed all the year round, tackling any farm work that did not involve horses. They would be paid about a third of a man's wage. What the women had in common were their wide straw bonnets. Sunbathing did not become fashionable till the twentieth century and the bonnets were designed to shield their faces from the sun.

A speech made by a sympathetic observer in 1849 suggests that the nature of agricultural work for women has not changed.

> I must here give some allusion to those females engaged in outwork; surely their work is far from desirable and far from effeminate. Many of these are hired at very low wages to pull turnips during the winter. Conceive a female having to work in the open air all day amidst drifting snow, drizzling sleet and drenching rain, and this day after day. Is this fit and proper work for a woman? ... Add to this, those engaged are of the poorest and are not able to procure for themselves anything like comfortable clothing.

Other sources of extra labour for harvesting were the Highlands and Ireland. Leaving work on the crofts to their womenfolk, the men often walked to the arable farms of the south and east where they were housed in bothies – rough accommodation somewhere about the steading – and usually fed in the farm kitchen. During the war most of them joined the armed forces and their places were taken by the Girls who worked in gangs.

In 1938 women's pay went up to two thirds of men's, but during the War the wives of farm labourers were unlikely to be employed since mothers with children under fourteen could not be called up. They were replaced by women who were childless, as were all Land Girls on recruitment. Like most of them I was an ignorant townie with romantic ideas about country life; unlike most of them I had considered farming as a career. But to be a farmer required an amount of capital which I knew my parents could not provide. For a degree in History I was sure they would find the money. Clearly, the degree was now going to have to wait.

By the 1940s farmers were realising that extra labour was essential. Many Scottish farmers were suspicious of women workers outside the dairy or the poultry yard but the Armstrongs were more broad-minded than most. They had been Border farmers for many generations. A large family, one of their daughters, my Girl Guide captain, had been a maths teacher, another was married to the local doctor and one of the sons was an accountant. In 1939, four of their sons were farming and Jack, the youngest, was in partnership with his father.

The Job

With a rainfall of fifty-eight inches, Galloway was ideal dairy country. Snow and frost rarely lasted and grass often grew for eleven months in the year. On adjoining farms the Armstrongs usually had over a hundred Ayrshire cows. At Littleton, the larger of the farms, they made cheese. My training started disastrously in the dairy. It was staffed by the dairyman and his wife and daughter. Milking started at 5am, cheesemaking after breakfast and the second milking about 4pm. Most of the cows would let down their milk to machines but the 'difficult' cows had to be hand-milked. By the end of the week every cow I had tried to milk had gone dry. The dairyman suggested that I should be moved to the stables: the cows and I were equally delighted.

There I was much happier. Horses keep more civilised hours than cows and we had always got on well together. There were five Clydesdales at Littleton, three at Townhead, and it was 1944 before the first of the tractors which were to replace them appeared. The thistle-cutting part of my training became much easier when I persuaded the men that I could manage a proper scythe better than the inefficient hook which was thought to be more appropriate for a girl.

But to the end of the War I depended on one of the men to sharpen my scythe.

One of the pleasures of a mixed farm is the variety of the work. I became the orraman, defined in the dictionary as 'a farm worker kept to do any odd job which might occur'. They usually worked on their own. I did most of the carting – hay, corn, turnips, dung and lime – and simple operations like drilling with one horse or harrowing with two. The men did the ploughing and, with three horses, drove the binder. I have ploughed, but would not claim to be a plough-woman. In my first summer I was entrusted with the hay rake, a simple horse-drawn rake which gathered cut grass into rows. These were 'coled' – drawn into small heaps manually – and a few days good drying would turn the grass into hay. This would be built into small stacks for further drying. Given a week of good weather, these would be carted to the steading, built into larger stacks and stored for winter feed. Inadequately dried grass would heat and moulder, ruining the hay. Silage, better suited to the Galloway climate, did not reach the Armstrongs' farms till after the War. A method of preserving grass which had been developed in the thirties, it required a pit in which to store the grass – the silo – and a tractor to provide the pressure necessary to exclude the air. Cut green, the grass was stored in the silo and each layer compressed by the tractor and sprayed with molasses. When full, the silo was covered with a plastic sheet weighed down by old tyres or earth. The smell was terrible but animals loved the end product. In the large black bags seen in the fields now, air has been excluded by the pressure of the baler. Silage has taken the place of hay as the main source of winter feed.

Haymaking in the west of Scotland will always be a gamble; so too is the harvest. Heavy summer rain can flatten the crop and lack of sunshine delay ripening. Wheat and barley were limited to the arable farms of the east. In the west the use of combine harvesters was delayed until efficient drying techniques had been developed, but the horse-drawn binder worked well, cutting and tying the oats into sheaves and throwing them clear of the machine. Before any reaping machine could operate, the old-fashioned scythe had to be brought into use to clear a path round the field. One of the men would scythe the crop growing on the head rig and two of us would follow him, gathering the cut corn into sheaves and binding them with their own straw. A squad of workers would then follow the binder, building the sheaves into stooks, usually eight to a stook. If the sun shone they might be ready for stacking in a week but too often it rained and the corn began to sprout. The increasingly bedraggled stooks then had to be moved, sometimes repeatedly, to let in dry air and the harvest could drag on till September. During hay and harvest we worked a sixty hour week – seven to six – without extra pay. From six to eight there would be overtime at ten pence an hour for a woman. Although we might have worked longer the horses couldn't. Unlike tractors, they had to have food and rest.

In time my horse and I were entrusted with more complicated operations. Loading a cart with hay or sheaves of corn was one of them. Wooden rails were added to the cart to create an extended area on which to carry relatively light crops. Fork loads were packed from the outside to the centre of the cart, always in a clockwise direction, and each layer had to be well-hearted before starting the next. A carefully built high load would survive the roughest track to the steading. The same method was used when building stacks in the yard. Thatched with straw, held down by ropes weighted with stones, they were virtually waterproof. Seventy years later, when researching the transfer of farming skills from Scotland to Poland in the nineteenth century, I discovered that at Phantassie, a farm near East Linton, aristocratic Polish landowners were being taught how to build stacks by the same method. Another skill I learned was the management of the triangle – a horse drawn pulley with which a small stack of hay could be lifted onto a cart. Careless handling of the horse could have led to disaster. And if the field were a long way from the steading, there could be a blissful ten-minute break before the arrival of the next cart. Optimistically, I always kept a book in the pocket of my battledress.

In the winter, foddering out-wintered sheep and cattle became one of my most important jobs. In every field there would be bins to store the feed and wooden troughs from which the animals were fed daily. This took me to the furthest reaches of the farm, some accessible only by steep roads. In icy weather these could be treacherous. As their hooves began to slip, most horses went more and more slowly until they finished up with their knees and the shafts of the cart on the ground. Not an easy situation to deal with on your own. In icy conditions I learnt to harness Blossom, the most nervous horse in the stable. As soon as she started to slip she went faster and often reached safety at the top of the hill.

Some of my happiest days were spent with Andy, the shepherd. The farms carried both beef cattle and sheep. These had to be counted every day and inspected for possible injuries or infestation of their rear ends by maggots. A sheep can become top-heavy and on its back or stuck in a hedge it has to be rescued. When Andy needed help it was for dipping and dosing the sheep and, in the spring, castrating the males and docking the tails of all the lambs. This made it easier to keep them clean and free from the flies and their maggots. With his highly intelligent Border Collie he would round up the sheep and bring them to the boughts, enclosed areas in which sheep can be easily handled. Catching and holding a blackface was easy; two nicely rounded horns gave you excellent handles to grab. Cheviots and Border Leicesters, hornless and short coated, were more difficult. They were more delicate than the blackfaces, who were bred for hill farms, and lambed earlier. I would hold the sheep while Andy carried out the necessary operations.

Dipping was always fun and shearing could become a social occasion if one or two men had been borrowed from a neighbouring farm. A team was needed to bring the sheep to the shearers and the fleeces to the men who packed them ready for sale to the wool merchants. There was always one man, armed with disinfectant, to render first-aid to the sheep. When I graduated from catching the sheep to shearing them I no longer saw myself as an unskilled worker. I discovered that shearing was much easier than it looks. The fleece rises at the end of the winter and, after a few clips, can be peeled off. If unsheared, it will eventually fall off, but it was only too easy to clip the sheep. This I knew was a disgrace and I had to resist the temptation not to call in the first-aider if I had injured my sheep.

I never stopped enjoying working with horses and other animals – time flew. What I often disliked was fieldwork when I had to stop myself from looking at my watch at the end of every drill. The work was usually endlessly repetitive, boring and often backbreaking. Hoeing turnips I positively hated – ten hours a day for what seemed like weeks in the early summer and midday dinner time was the only break. Acres of densely growing seedlings had to be singled in a period of a few weeks and other work on the farm was postponed until hoeing had been completed. Conscientious in the extreme, I frequently finished by knocking out the seedling I had decided should remain and, always the slowest in the squad, I would still be labouring away when the men had reached the end of their drills and were lighting up cigarettes. Pins and needles in my hands added to the misery. It was usually Andy who helped me to finish my drill and catch up with the men.

Shawing – pulling up the turnips and cutting off their leaves and roots – was spread over a longer period and winter hours were in any case limited by shorter daylight. But in midwinter the leaves could be covered with ice. In a few minutes my gloves would be soaked and my hands frozen. Emptying the midden and spreading dung over the fields was a heavy and not very pleasant job; eight horses and one hundred cows produce a lot of dung. But carting and spreading lime was worse. Heavy rainfall produces acid soils and a yearly application of lime is essential in order to neutralise the acidity. Carted out and dumped in small piles, it rapidly turned to a fine powder. Using a shovel, this had to be spread over the fields, burning my sweating face and hands. Another job for which protective clothing could and should have been provided.

Given good weather, hay and harvest were happy social occasions. Wives often joined their husbands in the fields, as did visiting friends and relations. I have a lasting memory of Col. Jamieson, the local landowner, and my father forking hay up to my cart and rather enjoying observing their relative inefficiency. One of my surviving letters describes a harvest scene in 1945 in which my father joined the usual workforce, already augmented by the families of the men and by Italian prisoners of war. He was strong but not skilled and one of the sheaves he aimed at the cart nearly knocked the builder off it. Even potato-picking could be fun when school children got their 'tattie holiday' and joined us in what was a less back-breaking job for them than for us. Mechanisation was still minimal and unskilled labour useful if not, like my father's, potentially dangerous.

For threshing, skilled labour was essential. Townhead had its own machine with which two of us threshed small quantities of corn throughout the winter. Originally powered by water it had been converted to electricity and, on dark mornings, threshing indoors made a pleasant start to the day. But at Littleton there had never been water power and several times a year a large steam-powered machine was hired from a contractor. Operated by two men, the farmer was expected to supply about eight more. Some of these would be borrowed, on a reciprocal basis, from neighbouring farmers. I can still see the disgust on the face of one neighbour when Jack, the farmer, when asked to lend a man, produced a Land Girl.

Threshing days were social occasions. To provide a splendid meal for all the workers a sheep would have had its throat cut. Strictly illegal, its death would be reported as natural – 'a braxy sheep killed by an intestinal disease and found behind a dyke'. Butchering had always been one of a farmer's many skills. My own memories of threshing days are mixed. There was one terrible day when smoke from the engine was blown back onto the mill, covering all of us with soot. I can still see the blackness of my hanky when I blew my nose. More happily, there was a day when Jack was cutting the strings which bound the sheaves before feeding them into the mill. I was forking them from the barn to the mill and got considerable pleasure from watching sweat pouring down his face as I speeded up the operation.

It was on a mill day that I discovered what a blood lust was. In theory an animal lover, I hated and feared rats. The men used to tease me about this. 'They'll gang up your troosers' – if I were wearing boots – and 'they'll gang doon your wellies' – if I weren't. And rats love farms. Confronted by one in the steading, if unobserved, I would stand still until it ran away; if men were around I would try to kill it with any available weapon. They ate the food we were labouring to produce and contaminated what they did not eat. I knew they should be killed. When, on a threshing day, we reached the bottom of a stack of corn twenty or thirty would shoot out from their final lair. Threshing stopped, everyone grabbed a fork and, encouraged by the barking of the wildly excited dogs, the massacre began. And I remember enjoying it.

A Dangerous Occupation?

Was farming a dangerous occupation? I don't remember any of the men having a serious accident, but the machines we used – threshers, bruisers and shredders – were potentially dangerous. It was only too easy to get clothes or hair caught in a machine and a Land Girl working in Fife was scalped when her hair was entangled in the elevator of a potato dresser. And the hedging knives and scythes with which we worked had to be very sharp. First aid was usually included in the training of Timber Jills but not in that of Land Girls.

I think farm work has become more dangerous since tractors replaced horses. On Scottish farms, rock is rarely far below the surface and few fields are flat. On Littleton there was only one field in which there was not a know – a rocky outcrop which could not be ploughed. Ploughing steep ground vertically leads to erosion and flooding and contouring is essential, but when drawn by a tractor heavy machinery is more likely to overturn than when drawn by horses. Animals will always be both powerful and unpredictable and hundreds of farmers have been killed or seriously injured by bulls with whom they had worked safely for years. Dairy bulls are notoriously dangerous so I kept out of their way and it was a Border Leicester ram who took me by surprise. I had noticed that the bin in the field in which he was out-wintered was becoming badly battered; I did not notice in time that, when topping it up one morning, my behind became his preferred target. I never turned my back on him again.

My other injuries were minor and usually my own fault. The largest and quietest of the mares once trod on my foot and kept her well shod hoof on my unprotected one for a painfully long time. A few days later, as a bridesmaid at my brother Tommy's wedding, I was struggling not to limp as I carried his bride's train up the aisle. More humiliating was the occasion when I was kicked by one of the horses. Unusually harsh weather had made ploughing impossible and had kept him in the stable for several weeks, unexercised and tied up in a narrow stall. Instead of the usual bucket of water, I decided I would take him down to the burn for a proper drink. Too lazy to put on a halter, I threw a rope over his neck and enjoyed watching him enjoy his drink. It was on the way back to the stable that he threw up his head, threw off the rope and caught my face with his flying hooves. Staunching the blood, I was creeping back to the farmhouse, having decided not to mention the accident in my weekly letter home, when I recognised my brother-in-law's motorbike. His regiment was stationed about twenty miles away in Wigtownshire and he had ridden over to take me out to dinner. My face recovered fairly rapidly; my confidence when working with the horses took longer.

Roads were narrow but petrol rationing kept traffic down and accidents were mercifully rare. At a sale on a farm about

ten miles from Townhead, Jack bought a fertiliser spreader
and a horse. Knowing my enthusiasm for horses, he drove
me over and left me to do the rest. The first problem was
getting them off the farm as the machine was a few feet
wider than the gate. Fortunately the horse proved biddable
and careful manoeuvring got us onto the road. This was
wide enough for two cars but not for a car and an outsize
machine. That we survived a ten mile series of blind corners
was sheer good luck. I was equally lucky on a twenty mile
ride to the Armstrongs' hill farm near Carsphairn. This was
stocked with blackface sheep whose lambs would be sent
down to Littleton for fattening before the autumn sales. For
haymaking, the manager needed a second horse and the
cheapest way of moving a horse is to ride it. Tolerable for
ten miles, sitting on a cart-horse's back becomes increasingly
painful for the rider so I walked the last five miles. We arrived
safely but it took several days for my behind to recover.

The accident which took me into hospital was entirely
my own fault. A Girl who had recently come to work on a
farm four miles from Littleton had no bike. So that we could
cycle together to a WLA meeting, I borrowed a bike from
the dairyman's daughter. Riding mine and holding hers, I set
off, forgetting that there was a steep hill between the two
farms. Several hours later I woke up in the cottage hospital.
Miraculously, the bikes were uninjured and so apparently
was I, but I must have started to behave in a very odd way
by the time we reached Kirkcudbright. Lying in bed in a
strange night-dress, with no idea of how or why I had got
there, I was more than a little worried. I decided that if I
could remember the date of the Treaty of Westphalia, which

1. The toughening process - swimming lessons in the Tummel.

2. Land Army Recruitment Poster

LEEDS GIRLS' HIGH SCHOOL
Grammar School Foundation

This card, awarded to

M. K. McLEOD

FORM S.C.

represents

A PRIZE FOR
SCHOOL CERTIFICATE RESULTS
1939
which, owing to the war,
has not been given.

L. P. Kirk.
Headmistress

3. The first casualty in my war - the prize I didn't get.

4. To protect their complexions from the sun, ladies carried parasols. Bondagers had to work with their hands and depended on specially designed bonnets to keep the sun off their faces.

5. Bondagers at work - bonnets apart, the harvest scene hadn't changed in a hundred years.

6. Farm labouring - the ideal.

7. The reality.

8. Hay Raking.

9. Randolph Schwabe's *Hoeing* was painted in 1918 but the boring
and finicky nature of the job hasn't changed.

10. One of the pre-war tractors which, on arable farms, were beginning to replace horses, but it was 1944 before one reached Littleton.

11. Littleton - a substantial nineteenth century house.

12. Jack and Agnes with their daughter Elizabeth at Townhead. She and her husband Robert Dodds now live at Littleton and their son and his wife at Townhead.

13. Mona on Horseback
My favourite recreation - Muir's saddle and the Tester's pony.

14. On the coast road to Kirkcudbright a prized herd of cattle, the Belted Galloways, were housed in a magnificent byre known locally as 'The Coo Cathedral'.

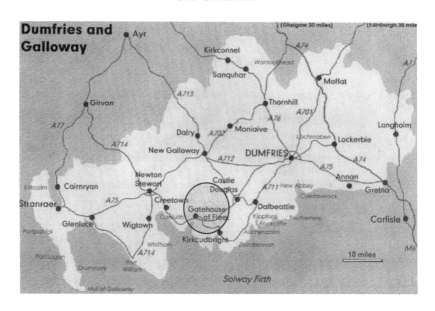

15. Map of Dumfries and Galloway

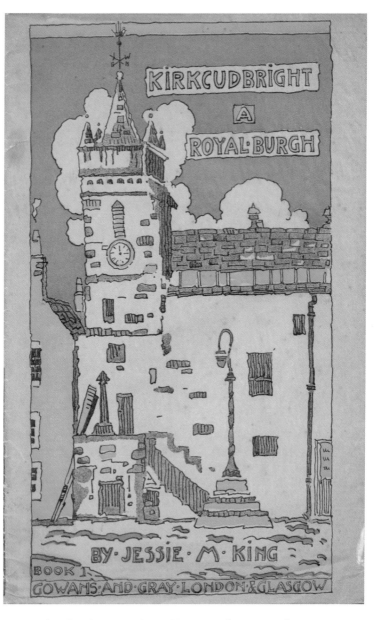

16. *Kirkcudbright; a Royal Burgh'* is one of my prized possessions.

ended Germany's seventeenth-century Wars of Religion, other memories would come back. 1648 came back but there is still a four hour gap between coming in from work on the Saturday morning and waking up in hospital.

Perhaps the greatest danger for a Land Girl was the heaviness of the work. Many of us were trying to prove that we could do anything a man could do. If it were a matter of skill we often could, but if real strength were required we couldn't. And, in the 1940s, men were expected to carry weights which I think would be unacceptable in the twenty-first century. Unloading lorries was an orraman's job. When feeding-stuffs and fertilisers were delivered they were usually in sacks weighing a hundredweight. The driver loaded them onto my back and I carried them to the shed in which they were to be stored. But basic slag came in deceptively small sacks which weighed a hundredweight and a half, far heavier than any woman, or man, should be expected to carry. By the end of the war my periods had stopped.

The Men

Were I to be marooned on a desert island and allowed one companion I would choose an old-fashioned farm labourer. Most were intelligent, resourceful, skilled in so many fields and very generous. After a month, language difficulties disappeared; I stopped noticing the broad Galloway accent and acquired a new vocabulary of farm terms. The men taught me all they could and helped me when I failed to master a skill. I never succeeded in sharpening a scythe or keeping up with the men during the miserable weeks spent hoeing turnips. Andy would help me to finish my row and Sandy, whose vocabulary was limited to swear words previously unknown to me and who might have been described as 'thick', never failed to move behind me when smoking his filthy smelling pipe. On the not infrequent occasions when Jack went off to the market in Castle Douglas, the men worked as steadily as when he was overseeing them. The only exception was Dave. One of the ploughmen, he was more likely to look for a quiet corner in which to enjoy a cigarette. When a tractor was acquired in 1944, driving it became his province and increased his sense of importance. But when I was taught to drive it his dislike of me was also increased. If Jack and he fell out, another not infrequent occurrence, I would be sent to drive the tractor. Early Fordsons had unpadded metal seats, metal wheels and no sheltering cab. Like early cars they had no starters and the cranks had a vicious kick. They were uncomfortable and noisy and, for the driver, could be incredibly cold. I retained my preference for horses.

The Italian prisoners employed towards the end of the war were excellent company. On some farms they became regular members of the staff and lived in the bothies but Jack only employed them at hay and harvest. He collected them from camps in Wigtownshire and returned them in time for their evening meal. I discovered that they were issued with dried fruits but were always short of cigarettes. These I could buy in the canteen and I knew that my mother needed fruit for the cake she was baking for my twenty-first birthday. A simple system of barter solved both our problems. When working they sometimes sang arias from the operas. I don't think I ever heard a Scottish farm labourer sing. I did, but only when driving a tractor so noisy that I couldn't hear my own voice.

Hours were long and pay abysmal. Until the twentieth century pay had been largely in kind, bargained for when the men were hired at the hiring fairs. These 'gains' had the advantage of being proof against inflation and often included a pigsty and grazing for a cow as well as coal, turnips and potatoes. The minimum wage for skilled agricultural workers, which came into force shortly before the War, was half the average wage of unskilled workers in other industries and women doing identical jobs were paid a third less than men. Land Girls were paid by the farmer, not the state, and came under the same legislation. In five years my pay, over and above my keep, went up from 12/6 to 30/- weekly. Inexplicably, Land Girls in England were marginally better off than those in Scotland; eighteen shillings with board and lodging was the minimum.

The married man's wage was £3. From this was subtracted a small sum for insurance against illness and unemployment and 5/- for a semi-detached cottage with a very small garden. Workers' cottages were tied to the jobs since a ploughman had to feed his horses before he had his own breakfast and the dairyman had to be near enough to the byre to hear a cow in labour. Villages were often miles from the farm, and farm labourers did not have cars. The Littleton cottages were two-roomed with stone floors, no electricity and no water. A few hundred yards up the road the farmhouse had both. The only 'gains' were a few potatoes, some coal and a daily quart of milk. Birth control was then almost unknown outside the upper classes, so families were often large and the meat ration, latterly just over a shilling a week per ration book, was beyond the means of many. From the butcher's van, which came round once a week, their wives would buy a few bones and enough meat for one or, at most, two meals. The rest of the time they ate porridge, soup and potatoes. In the farmhouse we had meat every day and must have been enjoying the rations the workers couldn't afford to buy. We were neither a poultry nor a pig farm, but the farmer's wife looked after a few hens and household scraps went to fatten a pig. Vegetables were grown in the kitchen garden and the eggs, cheese, butter, ham and bacon produced on the farm supplemented rationed food. High protein meals three times a day were the norm. I like porridge but the only time I was offered it for supper I must have expressed my indignation fairly clearly; it didn't happen again.

I was a student of social history before I discovered why farm workers – and Land Girls – were paid so badly. The Combination Laws, which in 1800 made it illegal for men to get together to discuss conditions of work, were applied to the employees but not to the employers. The farmers' societies which were founded all over Britain were successful in keeping wages down and hours up. A Tudor statute had made it legal for magistrates to enforce a living wage. They rarely did, but the statute was repealed in 1813 and it was 1825 before trade unions were legalised. Miners and factory workers who lived in close communities were then successful in reducing hours and securing a living wage; farm workers were not. Working on farms which were often small, widely scattered and isolated, and living in cottages which were without 'phones, they were unable to form strong unions. In tied cottages at a time when mechanisation was beginning to threaten employment they were at the mercy of their employers; wages remained low and hours long.

By the late nineteenth century an eight-hour day had become normal for many workers; for agricultural labourers it was still, in the 1940s, a minimum of ten in summer and eight and a half in winter. But animals don't have weekends. Horses had to be fed and watered and out-wintered sheep and cattle foddered on Saturdays and Sundays. The men and I compromised; they fed my horse on Saturday and Sunday nights and I fed theirs on Sunday mornings. During hay and harvest the farmer could demand an extra five hours of unpaid

Saturday afternoon work. We were all entitled to one week's holiday a year and what was left of New Year's Day after we had looked after the animals. Christmas was virtually ignored in Scotland. The 25th of December was a normal working day and in Gardenstown, the Banffshire village in which my husband and I lived in the 1950s, all the shops would be open. Celebrations were delayed till Hogmanay, when children got their presents and most people got drunk. It was 1958 before Christmas Day became a public holiday in Scotland.

At home, Christmas had always been the most exciting time in our year. My mother's family having spent most of the nineteenth century in Poland, celebrations started with a Christmas Eve supper. After presents round a candlelit tree, my father disguised as Santa Claus, we shared with my grandmother a Polish Christmas wafer and then sat down to the traditional 'fast' supper of borscht served with mashed potatoes, a very large fish with a delicious sauce and a salad made from dried fruits sent from Poland. On Christmas Day we became British again and stockings in the morning were followed by turkey and plum pudding at night. And the 25th was my birthday. I had to go home.

I knew that I was going to have to pluck up courage to ask for unpaid leave and would have to save up enough money for the return railway fare to Leeds. Every moment was precious. By the time I boarded the night train from Glasgow after the bus journey to Dumfries the train was always full. I don't remember a single journey in which I didn't have to join the servicemen sitting on their luggage in the corridors. My father would meet me in Leeds in the early hours of the morning and carry my case up the steep hill to our home.

Board and Lodging

My first year was spent at Littleton, a substantial nineteenth -century farmhouse and the home of Mr and Mrs Armstrong. During the War farming was subsidised and, like many other farmers, they were able to buy a farm which had previously been rented. Mr Armstrong had recently had a mild stroke and was semi-retired, so the pace was fairly gentle. Breakfast was at 7.30am and I had a room of my own with a bed not a bunk. It was unheated but so were most bedrooms at that time, and at least I didn't have to share it with other girls as those working in gangs often did. I was told to put my dirty clothes into the general laundry basket and they were returned to my room, washed and ironed. My older siblings had had to sit driving tests but these were suspended during the War and Mr Armstrong began to teach me to drive. I was treated as a member of the family, but the resident maid, her room up a backstair, was not. Her social life was elsewhere; within a few months of my arrival she became pregnant and disappeared.

For wartime, food was splendid: porridge, bacon, eggs and scones for breakfast; meat, potatoes and a second vegetable followed by a pudding for dinner. This was usually a milk pudding, much improved by stewed fruit and the pint of cream which came from the dairy every morning. High tea would be a protein dish followed by more scones. The family had an early meal in the sitting room and I ate mine alone in the kitchen when I came in from work, enjoying the chance to read one of the many excellent books published by Penguin at the affordable price of sixpence.

The men carried flasks for their tea breaks; I was too lacking in confidence to ask for one. But I was rarely thirsty and never carried water. In winter, thirst could be quenched by a slice off a swede turnip and it was only during hay and harvest, when we were working till 8pm, that there was an official break. The farmer's wife would bring out tea for all of us; a basket of scones, one half filled with cheese and the other with jam, and a large can of tea. Any spares I ate.

By the time I had washed, changed and eaten my supper, evenings were short. During the summer I sometimes spent time in my room trying to identify the flowers I had found in the fields. Before I left home my father who, as a medical student, had studied materia medica, lent me his botanical textbook and my mother, knowing that I loved arranging flowers, had given me a pewter measure, perfect for small arrangements. Except in the hardest of winters this could be filled with wildflowers, though gorse, the only winter flowerer, was definitely difficult to handle. Flowers became an essential part of my life. Enjoying in old age the luxury of wine with my dinner and flowers in my sitting room, I know that if one had to go it would have to be the wine.

After midday dinner the only heating in the farmhouse was in the sitting room, so most evenings were spent there

reading, writing letters and endlessly darning my knee-length
woollen stockings. The Armstrongs' evening visitors were
almost always relations. Conversation was usually limited
to the weather and the prices recently offered at the local
markets. Playing cards provided the chief entertainment. My
whist was as bad as my milking, so I would tuck myself into
a corner and try to read until it was time to help with the
passing round of scones and cakes. Apart from washing up
my own supper dishes, unlike many Land Girls, I was never
asked to do housework. Although strictly against the rules,
many Land Girls were. The one time I was told to weed
the drive to Littleton's seldom-used front door I was deeply
resentful. I had not joined the Land Army to weed drives.

When Mr Armstrong had another more serious stroke,
my room was needed for a resident nurse and I was moved
to Townhead, their neighbouring farm. This must have been
very hard for Jack and Agnes. Fairly recently married, the
last thing they would have wanted was a brash eighteen-
year-old living on top of them. Life became tougher for me
too. Breakfast at 6.30am or 7am became the norm, as did a
longer working day and having to launder my own clothes.
The kitchen fire, which heated the water, was allowed to go
out after midday dinner so both the water and the kitchen
were cold by the evening. Saturday afternoon was the only
time I could have a hot bath. But I was always treated with
kindness. Jack usually fell asleep over the *Glasgow Herald*
soon after supper but Agnes read books as well as the
papers and shared my enjoyment of radio programmes like
The Brains Trust. One of the most successful of the BBC's
wartime programmes, this was one in which Professor

Joad, a populariser of philosophy, Commander Campbell, a down-to-earth naval officer, and writers like Janet Adam-Smith and J.B. Priestly would discuss plays, exhibitions and recently published books. On the advice of a professor at Leeds University I had tried to keep up my interest in history by reading the textbooks he had recommended, but this was not a great success. Ten hours of physical work and a large supper are not a good preparation for academic work. Babysitting was not an approved occupation for a Land Girl but I welcomed the occasional change from work out of doors which made it possible for Agnes to get to Castle Douglas for the Monday market or enjoy an evening visit to friends. Their only attempt at a holiday was a failure. After four days away from the farm Jack was so bored that they came home. I was disappointed.

Social Life - Year One

For the first year social life outside the farmhouse was almost non-existent. However well I got on with the men, I was never invited into their homes. Living with the family in the farmhouse was a 'them and us' situation and I was definitely one of them. In the steading we were social equals. We met every morning in the stable, where Jack gave us our orders for the day, and again at midday. The horses had to be given time to digest their meal, so we all had an hour's rest. In the evening they had to be set up for the night: groomed, given fresh straw to sleep on and bruised oats, chopped turnips and hay to eat. Sugar was rationed and the molasses used to make the oats more appetising for the horses helped to produce excellent gingerbreads in the farm kitchen. In the summer after a long day's work, taking the horses out to graze was for all of us one of the happiest times. They galloped round the field, rolled on their backs and, unlike the sheep, knew how to get back on their feet again. The stable was the social centre of the farm.

Gatehouse of Fleet was the nearest village. Developing round textile factories in the early eighteenth century, it reverted to a substantial agricultural village when steam

replaced water power and industries moved nearer to the
coalfields of the Central Belt. By the 1930s the Murrays, the
local landowners, had moved to one of their farmhouses
up the glen and their mansion house had become the Caly
Palace Hotel. During the War it was requisitioned for one
of the Glasgow girls' schools. Gatehouse also boasted a
church, two good small hotels, a row of shops, a primary
school, a resident doctor and a village hall. I am sure there
were regular Friday night dances there to which I might have
gone, but I was alone and socially nervous. I had grown up
observing my sister Lilias, six years my senior and a medical
student at Leeds University, not going to dances but being
taken to them. Her partner would call for her, be introduced
to our parents and return her at an acceptable hour. I braved
a village dance only once; an unforgettable experience. I had
not yet discovered the attractions of lipstick but, dressed in
my best dress, I joined the women sitting at one side of the
hall, ready to be inspected by the men on the opposite side.
When and if chosen, one of them would take you through
the dance, abandon you in the middle of the floor and leave
you to return to your place amongst the women. I love
dancing but decided not to repeat the experience.

Fortunately, the hall had other uses. On moonlit nights
when cycling without lights was relatively safe, there was
the Women's Rural Institute. Not the most inspiring of
institutions, but just to be out amongst people not connected
with the farm was exciting. Competitions were appropriately
domestic and rural – prizes for the best drop scones, the
fastest peeled potato, or the largest number of objects which
could be packed into a matchbox. Whist drives were more

exciting. There were always a few tables at the far end of the hall for Beetle Drivers – those who couldn't play whist – and then tea, scones and cakes for everybody. I was always hungry. During the War my father only allowed himself one week's holiday. When my parents came up every summer to spend it at the Anwoth Hotel, I used to eat my high tea at 6pm, wash, change and cycle down to Gatehouse in time to eat a full three course dinner at 7.30pm. At 9.30pm tea and cakes were ordered to fortify me for the uphill return to Townhead. Eating a full breakfast at 6.30am the next morning never produced any problems.

I missed my family most at the weekends. At home there were too many obligatory religious services on Sundays, but there had always been a formal tea party in the afternoon. To this, postgraduate students of many nations and colours were invited and the world and its problems discussed. After dinner on Saturdays our father often read to us. John Buchan, R.L.Stevenson and Mark Twain were the favourite novelists and on Sundays it would be biographies or essays. Those of us who left home during the war were kept in touch with the family by my father's weekly letters. These continued until we both lived in Edinburgh, he in his eighties and I in my forties. My mother wrote articles and occasionally lectured but wrote fewer letters. Graduating from Glasgow University in 1912 and marrying in 1914, she was of a generation of women who did not expect to combine a career with marriage.

On the farm, weekends were helped by the many people who took pity on a lonely Land Girl. The minister and his wife, who lived about four miles away, were amongst those

who invited me to knock on their door any evening. He was
unusual in that he farmed the thirty acres or so of the glebe
land which still provided part of the income of country
parish ministers. Most of them let this out to neighbouring
farmers. He told me that he was criticised for spending too
much time on his farm while those ministers who let out
their land were criticised for their lack of interest in farming.
For as long as I could sustain it, we talked farming. They had
a baby and I knew that after I had enquired for her health
no other subject of conversation would be possible. I was
not yet interested in babies. In Borgue, a village about six
miles from the farm, I got to know two very friendly 'elderly
spinsters' – probably in their forties at the time. They gave me
tea and lent me some of the books with which their house
seemed to be filled. But the most exciting experience socially
was dinner with the Jamiesons, the local laird and his wife.
Accustomed to the comfort of trousers and boots, I would
dress with great care and then suffer the misery of a rolling
up roll-on. Replacing the corsets in which my mother's
generation had been imprisoned, it was a wide elastic belt
designed to suppress our stomachs and buttocks and hold up
our stockings. Discomfort would be increased by my first gin
and tonics. I later discovered that gin does not agree with me
but I felt that, being invited out to dinner, I had really grown
up and that pre-dinner drinks were an essential part of the
experience.

Kirkcudbright was the nearest town. Land Girls were
often excluded from NAAFI canteens but the canteen in
Kirkcudbright was run by the parish church, originally for
men from the Air Sea Rescue Station at the mouth of the

River Dee. The Minister, the Rev James Nicol, reported to the presbytery:

> Some time ago a messenger came up to the Manse to tell
> him that there were some Land Girls in the local canteen
> and enquiring what should be done about them. One
> pictured a monstrous regiment of women in the place but
> actually, when he went down, there were only a few girls.

I was probably one of them. It was essential, both for my morale and the Armstrongs', that I should not spend my weekends 'relaxing' around the farmhouse. The canteen was the only place where I could find food at an affordable price and meet men of my own generation. It became my weekend home, well worth the eighteen-mile round trip. Treasuring the packet of Woodbines which would have to see me through the week, I cycled back to the farm, moon or no moon, my sweater reeking from the smoke-filled atmosphere of the canteen. We all smoked. Tormented by flies I had discovered that smoking discouraged them and gave me an excuse to stop working while I lit up. It also helped socially; 'lighting up' broke the ice for a very naïve young woman. During the war and for some time after it cigarettes were difficult to get but service canteens were more generously stocked than local shops.

The smoking problem was solved during my university years by an acute shortage of cash. Though eligible as an ex-servicewoman for a grant it was far from generous. Topped up by my father it covered the bare necessities, but to have bought a drink would have been unthinkable. In my first year British Restaurants, set up during the War, were still serving soup and a piece of bread for two pence and steamed pudding with phoney custard for four. My midday meal cost me sixpence. In 1946, the Restaurants closed and lunch in the Women's Union cost a lot more. I expect the Men's Union would have charged much the same but, except for the Friday night hops, it was closed to us, as our Union was to them. My income became increasingly inadequate. I was going to have to give up either coffee or cigarettes. Coffee was essential to keep me awake for late night work so cigarettes went. A lucky escape. It was many years later before the severe damage caused by smoking was recognised.

The other great attraction of Kirkcudbright was that it had become the home of a community of artists. I discovered this through Dorothy and Bill Johnstone's craft shop, the outlet for woodwork, pottery, jewellery and the pictures of other artists as well as for their own. They too took pity on me and invited me for tea in the room behind the shop. Through them I met other artists including E.A.Taylor and Jessie M. King. As I was still a golden blonde she called me Corn McLeod and gave me a signed copy of her beautifully illustrated book, 'Kirkcudbright'. Another growing up moment!

After the War I joined the Johnstone's three student children in their Edinburgh house. Potentially an artist, an architect and a doctor , they were all starting the academic training which had been delayed by the war. A housekeeper cooked our breakfasts and high teas and I discovered the reality of the rationing of food and the shortage of fuel. I had not lost my appetite and could tell the time, sitting in a lecture room, by the rumblings of my tummy – 11am if breakfast had been porridge, 12 noon after bacon. The winters of 1945 and '46 were exceptionally cold. Back into short skirts and silk stockings I froze, hands too cold to take notes without gloves and too clumsy with them. In the unheated north-facing room in my digs, it would be after 9pm before the coal fire I had lit at 6pm made it possible to remove some of the hot-water bottles and blankets which had made academic work possible. The post-war years were wonderfully exciting but not memorable for creature comforts. The Johnstones' wedding present, Dorothy's *A Blue Day at Carrick*, still hangs in my bedroom, reminding me of their many kindnesses as well as the beauty of the Galloway coast.

Social Life – Years Two to Five

In the introduction to her excellent book on the WLA, Victoria Sackville-West wrote 'We are tired of hearing the WLA referred to as the Cinderella of the women's services.' Reading this in 1944 it was difficult not to conclude that this was even more true of the Scottish Women's Land Army. Of the 80,000 Land Girls in the UK only 8,500 were in Scotland and, for once, I had to admit that there might be advantages in working in England. Her richer soil and gentler climate made arable farming the norm. Labour intensive, it could employ far more girls per acre and there was an incentive to provide monthly newsletters, instruction books like *Land Girls: a Manual for Volunteers to the WLA* or the clubs of which, in Scotland, we had never even heard. Subsidised by the government, the 600 clubs in England and Wales were often supplied with games, radios and pianos. Hostels were encouraged to act as social centres for Girls working on neighbouring farms and, in much of England, Girls were rarely far from a village and a bus route. No one I knew had even heard of the correspondence courses in agriculture and horticulture which Girls in England were encouraged to take. In theory their pay, conditions of work and general welfare were checked every month by the local Representative. No one I knew received such a visit, though I am sure that had I complained my complaint would have been investigated.

By 1943 numbers in Galloway peaked at 235; in Orkney at six. Ayrshire was the only county in Scotland with as many as 1,000 Land Girls; in England there were thirty counties with more than 1,000 Girls and in Yorkshire there were over 4,000. In theory conditions were the same throughout Britain, but south of the Border the WLA was an independent organisation run from her home by Lady Denman. There was no Lady Denman to represent us at the Department of Agriculture in Edinburgh. Perhaps it was as well that we were unaware of the amenities which were available in England but failed to cross the Border.

It was nine months after I joined the WLA before I met another Land Girl. In the spring of 1941, Mrs Grierson, the county organiser, gave a tea party for Girls within reach of Kirkcudbright. In the surviving photo there are only five of us. Doris, who worked on a small holding near Gatehouse, was only a few miles from Townhead, but the small group who became close friends were often much further away, nearer to Castle Douglas. We all worked on isolated farms and met at weekends if we had the energy for the long cycle rides involved. The most memorable weekend was spent at the home of Hilary, who worked on her parents' farm and had really rideable horses. When she married a Northumberland landowner after the War, she rode them over the Border to their new home – an unusual trousseau. A few days before the 1945 election her father, very much a 'gentleman farmer', was chairing a meeting for the Conservative candidate. From the back of the village hall Hilary and I barracked. Her father was not amused.

It was 1943 before the National Farmers' Union petitioned the Agricultural Executive to establish a hostel in Castle Douglas. Two were set up, but I never met any of the Girls who lived in them and worked in gangs. Most of us were almost totally isolated and Doris, the only employee of an elderly couple, went into clinical depression. The rest of us survived. And in 1945 my sister Mary, too young at seventeen to start her nursing training at Edinburgh Royal Infirmary, joined me. Owners of smallholdings who had previously produced fruit, flowers and vegetables for home consumption were allowed to employ Land Girls if food replaced flowers and two thirds of the produce went to the market. The smallholding on which she worked – goats, hens and market gardening – was only five miles away from Townhead and her employer, the widow of an admiral, had a house full of books, dogs and fleas. Fleas were a small price to pay for the level of the conversation, and Mary's company transformed my weekends.

One of the most memorable was spent on the moorland slopes of Cairnsmore of Fleet, hunting feral goats. Until the nineteenth century, goats had been the main source of milk. When improved transport made large-scale dairy farming profitable, they were replaced by cows and the goats were turned loose. Like the deer, in hard weather they came down from the hills and raided the pastures of low lying farms. Some of those we rounded up were killed immediately and others fattened for future consumption. A surviving letter describes returning from the hunt with Roger Armstrong, two of the farm men and, in the back of the Land Rover, one dead and one living goat. Mary and I sent our share of the kill to our parents to augment their meagre meat ration. It cost my mother her cleaning woman. Offered roast goat for dinner, she said she had never before been asked to eat anything so disgusting. She did not come back. My breeches had to be sent to the cleaners: alive or dead, goats have a powerful smell.

A few weeks later we celebrated VE Day together, cycling a long sixty miles to spend the weekend with a cousin of my father's who lived in Wigtownshire. A widow, she was managing a small textile factory which belonged to her family. While other people lit bonfires and set off fireworks to celebrate the defeat of the Germans, we explored the mysteries of a factory which produced tweeds and blankets.

Bicycles were our salvation. In England they might be provided by the WLA or hired for a shilling a week, but we had to find our own. My father bought an excellent one for me, old-fashioned, second-hand and gearless, but sturdy and reliable. Mary's, geared but a late wartime model, was neither. Alone, I had started to explore the country around the farm; now, with friends, I went further afield. Roads were empty and the country we explored was beautiful. The Carrick shore was our favourite haunt. Washed by the Gulf Stream, it was rich in flowers, many of them rare and, when the tide was in, the Solway Firth was good for swimming.

Any time there was a rideable horse at the farm I rode it. Not all the horses were heavyweight pure-bred Clydesdales and once a month there was the Milk Tester's pony. Employed by the Milk Marketing Board, he assessed the quantity and quality of milk being produced by every cow on every dairy farm in the county. A poor producer would be ejected from the herd. Less welcome was the man who could arrive any morning to check the butter-fat and water content of the previous night's milking. Ayrshire cows produce good milk and, from over sixty cows, the pint of cream lifted every morning for consumption in the farmhouse would not be registered. But water – from a leaky cooler? – would. 'Damn it,' said Jack, 'Ah didna' think they'd come on the sabbath'.

The Tester always spent the night at the farm and allowed me to ride his pony. One of Mrs Grierson's sons had lent me a saddle so, flourishing an elegant crop, a present from my grandmother and one of my most prized possessions, I cantered over the fields and forgot about hoeing turnips. Monthly visits to the smiddy, usually riding one of the Clydesdales and leading two more, was less exciting than riding the Tester's pony but, on a working day, as good as a holiday. The wife of one of the blacksmiths always gave me a cup of tea while the men shod my horses. Years later Jack told me that this enabled the men to revert, thankfully, to their normal vocabulary.

As children we had often been taken to see the sheepdog trials at Pitlochry. Bred for intelligence, not looks, they can control a herd and, at a word or a whistle from their master, separate the sheep he wants to handle from the rest of the flock. On the farm I never had a dog. Jack's collie was kennelled in the garage, lived on porridge and milk and never entered the house. He scarcely knew me and I would not have known how to control him. Dogless, I was once sent to Gatehouse to bring up six stirks – young cattle – to

Townhead. The first two miles were on the main road but there was very little traffic. All went well until a convoy of lorries driven by American GIs caught up with me. The GIs enjoyed the ensuing panic: I didn't. It was my only contact with the American forces.

Only one of my wartime friends was married, and potentially marriageable men were thin on the ground. I think I met four in five years and none were one of those farmers' sons with whom, in recent TV programmes, Land Girls in England seem to have spent most of the war rolling in the hay. My sex education had been minimal. Leaving home for the first time, my mother warned me against the dangers of accepting chocolate from a man while on the train journey to Scotland or allowing one to hold my hand at any time. The nature of the danger was not explained. No one had offered me chocolate on the journey north and it was many months before I obediently rejected the hand of Muir, the first man to try to take mine. But I had not been warned against the dangers of accepting loans and Muir had leant me the saddle which, for me, made riding possible. It was sitting on the saddle of my future husband's motorbike that I first got to know him.

Norman was a Glaswegian. At school he had planned to study agriculture but when his brother, a pilot, was killed he volunteered for the Navy. To fill in the months before he was called up, he came to work as a mud student at Culreoch, the farm of Jack's brother Roger, six miles up the Water of Fleet. At the end of a day when I had been sent to help with the threshing, Norman was asked by Roger to take me back to Littleton on his motorbike. I neither fell off the saddle nor clutched him in an unacceptable way. A keen mountaineer, he discovered that I had climbed some of the Perthshire hills and I think saw me as a possible partner. When his call-up papers came he passed on to me his subscription to Readers Union. For five shillings a month, a sum which even I could just afford, carefully chosen and recently published books came through the post. They kept me intellectually alive.

As children we had been introduced to the hills wearing short skirts and our school walking shoes. During a weekend when he was on leave, Norman introduced me to rock climbing on the Cobbler. Not far from Glasgow it is a hill rather than a mountain, not very high but with some excellent rock. In breeches and a pair of Norman's climbing boots, no longer waterproof but still well nailed, I discovered the joy of not slipping on slippery rock. Carefully roped and led, I reached the summit by an excitingly exposed route. At university I joined the Mountaineering Club and developed my rock climbing skills on Salisbury Crags. This was officially forbidden, but we discovered that park wardens were slow to come on duty on Sunday mornings. Many years later, when I joined the Ladies Scottish Climbing Club, I discovered that their founder members in 1907 had also developed their climbing skills on Salisbury Crags, but in long skirts. Climbing on rock, snow and ice, at home and abroad, kept our marriage alive for over twenty years.

It was July 1946 before Norman was demobilised. From submarines in the Mediterranean, he had been moved to a salvage vessel in the Pacific which was still clearing ships that had been sunk by the Japanese to block the harbours they had occupied. It was a year after their defeat before most of these became usable.

Letters had kept our relationship alive. Engaged by post, we married two years later, a week after my graduation from Edinburgh University. Ex-service students could graduate with an Ordinary degree in two years and an Honours in three. Tired of waiting, I had the distinction of graduating in three years with an un-classed Honours degree in History. I was assured that I could return to complete the degree at any time. The time has now come but the message from my brain is only too clear: too late, too late.

The Gangs

Two thirds of Scotland's land is designated 'harsh' – virtually uncultivable. Heavy rainfall and acid soil make much of the rest suitable only for stock raising and dairy farming, and there were few Land Girls north of Perth and the Highland Line. It is only in the east, where rainfall is low and hours of sunshine high, that there is good arable land and farmers there had long employed seasonal labour. During the War the many itinerant labourers who were called up were often replaced by Land Girls working in gangs. Many years later, when I was living in East Lothian, surrounded by some of the best farmland in Europe, I discovered how totally different from mine their experience of life in the WLA must have been. I can only quote from their own descriptions. Isabella Ranken, an Edinburgh Girl, was billeted at Quarry Court, near North Berwick.

'I enjoyed Quarry Court… we had dates with everybody… Polish lads, army boys, RAF… invitations everywhere. There was a NAAFI on the ground floor of Haddington Town Hall – a café… and upstairs was the local hop… The best thing about being a Land Girl was the camaraderie of the hostel: the worst was the winter weather.'

Most of the girls were townies and better trained than I or any of my Galloway friends. At colleges like Auchincruive in Ayrshire or Craibstone in Aberdeenshire, they would have been introduced to fieldwork before being sent to work on farms which were often near enough to Edinburgh, Aberdeen or Glasgow to make weekends at home possible. This was the one aspect of their lives that I envied. The Representative failed to inform me that, living more than twenty miles from home, I was entitled to a week's holiday and a travel warrant every six months. But I had not been sent from Leeds to Gatehouse, so perhaps my entitlement had been cancelled. Time off for Christmas, a family wedding, or Norman's leaves involved careful saving for fares. A favour had to be asked of the farmer and pay would be docked.

The weather was the same for all of us, though wetter and warmer in the west, and drier and colder in the east. At Littleton, indoor work about the steading – sawing wood, cleaning harness, filling up rat holes – could be exhausted after two days of rain. The third day it would be a cheerful 'Grand growing day the day, Mona' from Mr Armstrong as I set out for a ten hour soaking.

But the work done by Girls in gangs was usually as different from mine as was their social life. Gangs are ideal for arable farming and horticulture, and the soil and climate of East Lothian are perfect for both. The ubiquitous turnips and hundreds of acres of potatoes, carrots, leeks and sprouts had to be planted, hoed and harvested for the markets of the Central Belt. Most of this is repetitive, boring and back-breaking work, the kind I most disliked, and going to so many different farms it would have been difficult to get to know either the animals or the men.

Another great difference was accommodation. In East Lothian it could vary from a hostel for eighty at Rosewell, with four girls to a room, to a hut near Humbie where there were twelve girls but only one bedroom. Bunk beds were normal. At Saltoun Hall the girls lived in the servants' basement, at Eagles Cairnie they enjoyed the second home of an Edinburgh judge in the winter but were moved back to huts in the summer. Discipline was usually imposed by a housekeeper; dinner at 5.30pm and lights out at 9.30pm or 10pm were probably not abnormal and their working days were often shorter than ours. Houses could be requisitioned for war work. Dye Cottage, the small eighteenth century shooting lodge in Berwickshire to which our parents retired in 1951, had been used to house bracken cutters from a Helensburgh boys' school.

I would have been miserable, hating the lack of privacy in hostels and the monotony of the work done by gangs; clearly a matter of temperament, many of the Girls loved it. This is how one of them described hoeing. 'There were jobs that we all enjoyed like hoeing... there was always a gang of us, men and girls, and there was always a lot of chat going on.' Ina Seaton, who was 21 when she was called up in 1943, was an Edinburgh girl. 'We thoroughly enjoyed ourselves. And we used to go to Gifford for the pictures twice a week, Wednesday and Saturday, and if we wern'a at home for the week-end we piled into the car and we went to the pictures and went to the chip shop. There would be a dance on the Friday night. It was great. I didn'a want to go home.' Isabella echoed Ina. 'In the daytime I sometimes wished I hadn't joined. I liked it best at night.' But Ina continued: 'I loved the work as well, nothing was too heavy. It was hard work but you didna' look on it as hard work 'cause it was a lot of laughing and fun and things like that. - - - It really was nice, working in the open air and knowing that you were helping in the war effort in your own way.' Most of England is arable land so gangs were much commoner than in Scotland.

The Timber Corps

The other hostel dwellers were the Lumber Jills. In 1939, 90% of the wood used in the UK was imported, most of it from Canada or the Baltic countries. The German U-boat campaign made it impossible for this to continue. Domestic consumption of wood during the War could be reduced – in the few houses built metal replaced wood – but timber had to be found for uses as essential as telegraph poles, pit props and railway sleepers, and charcoal was used for explosives, gas mask filters and smelting. By 1942 the situation had become critical and lumberjacks were brought over from Canada and Newfoundland. As in World War I a Timber Corps was set up to support their work. Of the 6,000 recruited, 4,900 worked in Scotland as a branch of the WLA. England had been importing wood since the sixteenth century and, recognising the imminence of war, the Government had bought 1,444,000 acres of land and planted trees on 434,000, but the timber would not be ripe for felling until long after the War was over. Scotland still had extensive woodlands in the Grampians and the Cairngorms.

When trees had to be felled in the shelter belts which protected their fields at Littleton and Townhead, the

Armstrongs employed two local woodmen. My horse and I would have a happy day as their assistant, pulling out the timber and dragging it to the nearest road. The work of the Timber Corps covered a far wider range of activities. But felling was mostly in the North, so it was long after the War before I met a Lumber Jill and discovered how varied their work had been.

In 2012, for the first time, an exhibition was set up in the War Museum at Edinburgh Castle to commemorate our contribution to the war effort. At the opening ceremony I represented the WLA, and May the Timber Corps. The eldest of seven children, she had left school when she was thirteen. In 1943 her father decided that she should give up her job so that her mother, who could have earned more, would be free to go out to work. May would have had to look after her six siblings. The idea did not appeal to her: life as depicted on recruiting posters for the Timber Corps did. Discovering that at sixteen she was under age – 'Ah just lied abut ma age' – and that seventeen-year-olds required parental consent – 'Ah just forged his signature.' Fortunately for her and others like her, the WLA did not ask for a birth certificate and she escaped from the family home in Glasgow. A real volunteer!

Training for the Timber Corps was essential. Though most Land Girls were townies, many of us had some experience of country life and had worked in stables if not in byres or pigsties. I had paid for my rides by mucking out stables and cleaning tack. Other than collecting kindling even countrywomen had rarely worked in the forests. One of the first training hostels was at Shamford Lodge, a large house near Brechin, which was surrounded by some of the trees which were to be felled. Here girls were introduced both to the theory and the practice of timber production. If unhappy after the first week they could leave; those who stayed on were helped to develop the muscles they would need to fell trees and handle timber as well as learning how to select and process the trees they felled. Estimating the volume and value of standing timber required special training as did the selection of trees which could be used as poles, so essential for telegraph poles, pit props and barriers to block the roads which might have been used by an invading German army. There are as many specialities in timber work as there are in farming. The men usually tackled the larger trees which the girls then trimmed, burning the rubbish and dragging out, with horses or tractors, the fallen wood. They cleared the undergrowth, burned the useless wood and sometimes ran the sawmills. The work was varied, skilled and potentially very dangerous. During training a girl was killed by a falling tree and a forester friend told me that he didn't know a single man who had worked in the woods and not had a serious injury. Training sometimes included a course in first aid.

For pole selection and 'Acquisition', very special training and special girls were required. Working in pairs they had to walk the woods, marking straight trunked trees which were reserved for poles, and estimating the height, volume and quality of other timber. After a long day, summer or winter, walking many miles in unknown woods and finding their way on country roads from which all signposts had been removed, they had to find accommodation at a price they could afford and some way of washing and drying their clothes. Evenings were often spent doing calculations based

· KIRKCVDBRIGHT·A·ROYAL·BVRGH ·

·A·BOOK·OF·DRAWINGS·
WITH·LETTERPRESS·BY·
·JESSIE·M·KING·

·THE·TOLBOOTH·

·TO··
L·T·M
1934

I·I GOWANS·AND·GRAY·LONDON & GLASGOW I·I

17. Signature page from the book *Kirkcudbright; A Royal Burgh*

18. At Mrs Grierson's Tea Party - no longer alone.

19. With Doris and Bobby on the Carrick shore, one of our favourite haunts.

20. Bobby worked on a dairy farm. After the war she returned to England and ran her father's farm.

21. A beautician, Jan could look attractive even in dungarees. The only one of my friends who was married, her husband was serving abroad.

22. Norman, a would-be farrmer, worked on Rodger Armstrong's farm while waiting for his call-up papers for the Navy.

23. The Cobbler, where Norman introduced me to nailed boots and winter climbing.

24. Recognition at last! The exhibition in the National War Museum at Edinburgh Castle and my first meeting with a Lumber Jill.

25. Work was varied but often heavy and potentially dangerous.

26. Evelyn Dunbar, an appointed War Artist in 1940, conveys in *Bedtime* the lack of privacy suffered by many of the girls living in hostels.

27. May and I

By this personal message I wish to express to you

MONA K. McLEOD .

my appreciation of your loyal and devoted service
as a member of the Women's Land Army from
16th July 1940   to   4th October 1945.
Your unsparing efforts at a time when the victory
of our cause depended on the utmost use of the
resources of our land have earned for you the
country's gratitude.

Elizabeth R

28. The Queen was the Patron of the WLA. Her letter was the only recognition we received at the end of the War. It was the year 2000 before we were invited to lay a wreath at the Cenotaph on Remembrance Day.

29. A sculpture near Fochabers unveiled by Prince Charles in 2012
to commemorate the work of the Land Army

- a deceptively jolly image of life as a Land Girl which this book seeks to correct.

Women's
Land Army

Women's
Timber Corps

....

The Government wishes to express to
you its profound gratitude for your
unsparing efforts as a loyal and devoted
member of the Women's Land Army/
Women's Timber Corps at a time when our country
depended upon you for its survival.

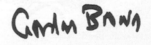

July
2008

Rt Hon Gordon Brown MP
Prime Minister

30. In 2008 Gordon Brown decided that we should be granted the medal
which has been denied us in 1945.

on the measurements they had made and making up reports on the day's work. Opportunities to meet other Girls and share in the social life which so many of them enjoyed would have been few and far between.

But most of the girls worked in large gangs. May enjoyed both the work and the company, but living conditions were usually tough. For the thirty Girls at Shamford Lodge they were described by one girl as 'Austere, everything was very cold, everything was minimal, comfort was minimal, a bath was a luxury.' In the huts in which twenty Girls lived conditions were even worse. Perhaps this was part of the training.

The first month of May's training was only moderately satisfactory. Not surprisingly, her father had pursued her to the hostel near Bridge of Orchy to which she had been sent. More surprisingly, he failed to get her home. Had he not known about the forged signature and the lie about her age? Her father returned to Glasgow and May settled down to two very happy years in the Timber Corps.

The warden of the hostel had been a nursing sister at Raigmore Hospital in Inverness, skilled at disciplining women but knowing nothing about forestry. May found herself amongst twenty Girls, most of them in their twenties and from very different backgrounds. Sadie, who became a lifelong friend, was the daughter of an Edinburgh dentist. May's father worked with ice; before the War very few people had refrigerators. Starting at 5am he delivered blocks of ice to fishmongers, restaurants and other businesses. He was grossly underpaid so May grew up in passed-on clothes and was humiliated, on her arrival at the hostel, to discover that she was the only girl without pyjamas.

Like mine, her training did not follow the model pattern – no lectures on the management of forests, no exercises to strengthen the muscles, no first aid. Accidents on site were dealt with by the lumberjacks. They seem to have been men of an exceptional calibre. One was a Norwegian and the three from Canada had been conscripted for work in Scotland. During the summer months they would be on site on the hillside at 7am. The girls joined them at 7.30am and were taught how to use axes and saws, how to trim or sned the fallen timber, how to burn the rubbish and how to drag out the timber with horses. It had then to be loaded onto tractors or lorries and driven to the saw mill at Bridge of Orchy. May never worked in a saw mill but was familiar with horses. They were still being used for transporting goods around the city centre when I lived in Glasgow in the early '50s. Organised by the Aberdeen police, a three month training in tractor and lorry driving came months later and driving then became her speciality. When the lumberjacks discovered how little the girls were paid they gave them money from their own wages

After their training most of the girls lived in huts near the woods in which they would be working. The Lodge, to which May was sent with five others, was exceptional. Its owner, Lady Seafield, remained in residence until her woods had been cleared. The girls lived in the servants' quarters and she made sure that they were as comfortable and as well fed as was possible with war time rationing. Every day of my five years living in a farm house I enjoyed as much meat, cheese and butter as I could eat. Timber Jills were limited to normal

rations and, doing heavy physical work – axes weighed four
and a half pounds and saws were six feet long – they must
frequently have been inadequately nourished and seriously
hungry.

Most of the girls learnt more from the lumberjacks and
old Scottish foresters with whom they worked than from
their official training. The huts in which they and the girls
lived were always near the woods but carefully separated, as
were those of the conscientious objectors and the prisoners
of war who often worked in the forests. Some of these were
quite aggressive, assuring the Girls that Germany would
win the war and that photos of concentration camps were
faked – just Churchillian propaganda. The Girls made their
own social life and petrol could usually be found if there
were a week-end dance in the nearest village. As partners,
lumberjacks were as good as any soldier and dancing became
one of the passions of May's life.

Accommodation on the next move was less attractive. As
an escape from midges huts were tolerable in the summer
but bitterly cold in winter. To spend the day working with
potential firewood and the nights shivering in inadequately
heated huts must have been particularly frustrating. From the
comforts of The Lodge, May's gang was sent to Pityoulish
Camp near Aviemore. This is how Ina, one of its inmates,
describes it:

'It used tae be an army camp and had just been vacated by
the army. All it was was wooden huts, just army wooden
huts. Another hut, a bit away, was for ablutions. But the
toilet was just a hole in the ground with a box over it.
Water was cold . If you wanted hot water you had to fill

the boiler and stand and wait 'til it heated up or someone
else would take your water.'

They had been sent to one of the toughest areas in Britain
where soldiers from many regiments were being trained
for guerilla warfare. Men from the Highland Light Infantry
joined the lumberjacks as dancing partners. The contribution
to the war effort of the soldiers is commemorated on site;
that of the Timber Jacks and Jills is unrecorded.

I think I would have been saddened by the felling of so
many beautiful trees. I disliked loading lambs and stirks onto
the lorries that took them to the abattoirs, but at least we
didn't have to witness their deaths. But to many Lumber Jills
the successful felling of a tree was a triumph. This is how
Mary, another Glasgow Girl , describes it:

> 'There was something lovely about watching a tree felling.
> I canna' explain it really, you know, when you saw it just
> falling down and you knew that you had planned it to fall
> there, you know? You couldna' do it willy-nilly. You had
> them sorta' here and there - that that one fell here and that
> one fell there - but then you had to leave a space between
> so one between could be felled. I always think back on it
> when I think on a tree felling, when I think of a tree falling
> down, it was a lovely thing to see you know.'

Although brought up in town, May was familiar with
horses. They were still being used to transport and deliver
goods in the centre of the city when I was living in Glasgow
in the 1950s. From horses she moved to tractors. The training
course organised by the Aberdeen police licensed her to drive
tractors and small machines, and tractor driving became

her favourite job. The end of the War brought an end to work in the Timber Corps, but she soon found a job as a bus conductress and much enjoyed it. Our war experiences couldn't have been more different but I think that both of us were enriched by the variety of work we had done and the people we had worked with. And three years later we both married men who had been in the Navy.

The Seasons

The farm year starts in the spring. After a good harvest corn might be sown in the autumn, but more often seed time was in the spring. As soon as the ground was dry enough for ploughed land to be broken down to a friable tilth by discs or harrows corn was sown and the ground firmed by rolling. Corn was followed by turnips sown in drills, and rape. This was not the crop which now turns the Lothians a blazing yellow in the early summer, but a green crop which provided good grazing for the sheep later in the year. Planting potatoes was the only back-breaking job in the spring. Carefully selected seed potatoes had to be placed in drills and then covered by a second drilling. Grass was still sown by hand. A mixture of grasses and clover, it was part of a seven-year rotation. Rye grass and clover were the animals' favourites and were the first to disappear from pastures. After four years of grazing by sheep or cattle the impoverished pasture had to be ploughed up and replaced by arable crops. To maintain milk production calving has to go on all through the year but lambing is always in the spring. Cheviots and Border Leicesters lambed in March and blackface sheep, usually on higher and colder pastures where grass grew later, in April.

On hill farms ewes are sometimes in-wintered, but this was unusual in the 1940s. Sheep would be fed through the winter and brought nearer the steading for lambing. A ewe whose own lamb had died might be given one of a pair of twins to feed, the skin of her own lamb tied round the body of the stranger. Very delicate lambs would be brought into the warmth of the kitchen and bottle-fed. Many Girls were shepherdesses but this was usually a job for the farmer's wife and, sadly, not for me.

Spring often ended and summer began with several weeks of drought, but the rain always seemed to come just in time to start the corn growing. Hoeing, which could only be done in fine weather, was followed by haymaking, the first of the harvests. This was followed by sheep-shearing and the corn harvest. Too wet for wheat, oats have always been the main corn crop in the west of Scotland. An early ripening barley which can now be harvested in the west was not introduced until long after the War. Our one attempt to grow rye was disastrous. Taller than oats, the crop was flattened by torrential summer rain and was virtually unharvestable. July and August are often the wettest of months. Back to cutting thistles! In a good summer the stackyard would be full by the end of August; in a bad one, crops would often have been flattened before the harvest started and sheaves ruined by repeated shifting in a desperate attempt to dry the corn and stop it from sprouting.

In September the weather often improved. Lambs and beef cattle, fattened over the summer months were sent to market and turnips and then swedes would be ready for harvesting. Pulled and stored in shallow drills in the fields they were safe from moderate frost; for immediate consumption they were shawed, carted to the steading and fed to in-wintered cows and horses. Potatoes were stored in clamps. These were piles covered with straw and soil to protect them from the worst of winter weather. Sixty years later I saw identical clamps in Poland. Near a village in the north east called Nowa Szkocja where, in the 1820s, Scottish farmers had introduced both the crop and the method of storing it, potatoes have become the usual ingredient in the distilling of vodka. Scottish drinking habits were also introduced. The only region in Poland where vodka is normally followed by a chaser is around Nova Szkocja.

Preparing the land for the next year's seed time started as soon as a crop had been harvested and ploughing continued throughout the winter. Hard frost or snow would have made this impossible, but in Galloway, near the sea and the Gulf Stream, arctic conditions rarely last. Roads leading to dairy farms would be rapidly cleared in order to rescue milk normally collected by lorry in the early morning. By November cows, calves and horses would be in-wintered, requiring endless care and attention. Horses went out to work and cows, in mild weather, to graze, but both ate and slept under the shelter of stable or byre. Sheep and beef cattle depended on the shelter of trees and the rations of oats and hay which had to be taken out to them daily. Shepherds looked after their welfare, ploughmen ploughed and orramen fed the out-wintered animals and continued to do the odd jobs around the farm.

Maintenance work was carried out during quiet periods throughout the farming year. Although farming was still relatively unmechanised there were already many machines that had to be cleaned, repaired and oiled before being stored for the winter. The men did the minor repairs, trained engineers the more serious.

Heavy rainfall made drainage of the land essential and the invention of tile drains in the early nineteenth century made this possible. Thousands of acres of land, previously bog, had been brought into cultivation. Laid in very shallow ditches, the tiles rapidly become clogged and should be lifted and cleaned every year. Dykes also require constant maintenance. When farms were enclosed in the eighteenth century, the stones lifted off the land were used to build the drystane dykes. Two hundred years later stones are still coming to the surface and have to be lifted off the fields. When the dykes had to be rebuilt professional dykers were employed but minor repairs were done by the men. Working from opposite sides, I learnt how to heart the dyke with small stones while the men built it up with the larger ones. By the twentieth century walls had often been replaced by deep ditches and thorn hedges. The ditches had to be cleared and the hedges trimmed. Untrimmed they become unnecessarily tall and thick at the top and very thin at the base, making it far too easy for stock to force a way through. And the wire fences which had often replaced hedges seemed to be in constant need of repair. A more recent innovation was the electric fence. These were used to divide fields where sheep were grazing on turnips or rape, preventing them from damaging and soiling the whole crop before they had cleared a restricted area. They had to be moved frequently. The only maintenance work which I did on my own and very much enjoyed was painting the carts.

These had to be washed and painted every year and fine weather was essential. Traditionally green and a very dreary red, I persuaded Jack to let me replace the red with a more cheerful orange. But this was a summer job.

The control of vermin was a major task. Killing the rabbits that flourished on the farm was one of the farmer's jobs. He shot them. We tackled the rats. In the 1940s there were more rats than people in Britain and each rat was believed to eat a hundredweight of food every year. Unfortunately they particularly liked corn crops, the source of our bread and porridge. A farm steading must have been their idea of heaven. In England over 1,000 Girls were trained to exterminate both rabbits and rats by gassing and poisoning, but the rat catchers Jack employed were certainly not Girls. One of our jobs, during quiet spells in the winter, was to fill up the holes through which they entered supposedly rat-proof areas. To fill these with cement was useless – the rats would have scraped it away long before it had had time to set. By adding broken glass to the mixture we succeeded in discouraging them, but as long as there is food around there will be rats. They are highly intelligent.

Together we maintained the structure of the farm – hedging, ditching, draining and dyking, servicing machines and painting the woodwork around the steading – but sowing, planting and harvesting always took precedence.

The War Experience

As the War dragged on I realised that although there had been no dancing for me, I had escaped its horrors. I had never heard a bomb or witnessed a death. When a Ranger company was founded in Gatehouse in 1944, I joined for purely social reasons and then discovered that Rangers, Girl Guides over sixteen, were being trained for relief work in post-war Europe. I volunteered. Training was minimal. It was suggested that we should practice sleeping on the floor and learn the language of one of the devastated countries to which we might be sent. After a week I decided that sleepless nights on the bare boards of my bedroom were damaging my contribution to the war effort so I got back into bed. An attempt to learn Polish was equally unsuccessful but I enjoyed a weekend in Edinburgh; interesting lectures; dragging our camping gear along Princes Street; spending the night by the sea, in the grounds of Gosford House. But when the war ended I was told that, at twenty-two, I was too young for relief work abroad. It was 1950 before the WLA was dissolved, but I was given immediate release to take up my university place.

I was the only member of my family, all volunteers, to be demobbed before 1946. Their wartime experiences had been very different from mine. My oldest sister Lilias completed her medical degree, married and worked in London till Dick, her first husband was demobilised. A keen OTC boy, he had joined the Territorial Army when he went up to Cambridge and was in camp when war broke out. Rapidly promoted, he was reputed to be the youngest colonel in the British army and was posted to Combined Operations, the planners of D Day. It was to be within reach of Camberley, where he was stationed, that Lilias moved to London. My brother Tommy volunteered for the Marines as soon as war broke out and worked as a very junior assistant in my father's laboratory until his call-up papers came through. In charge of anti-aircraft guns, unlike many young infantry officers, he rarely saw the men for whom he was responsible killed or injured and never saw the men killed by his guns. It was October 1946 before, with a wife and two children, he could return to Cambridge. My brother-in-law Rorie was a professional soldier. His Division, the 51st, was left to protect the retreat of the British army to Dunkirk. He occupied his five years as a prisoner of war writing a history of the Highlands. Officers in prison camps were not made to do manual work and the Red Cross was often successful in providing them with books. Like me, my sister Catriona was still at school when war broke out. After a year as a technician in the newly formed Blood Transfusion Service she joined the ATS. She remembers her years in Kenya as socially the best in her life. She was one of about thirty girls for whose company several hundred officers queued up; St. Andrew's University in 1946 was much less lively. Robert, my second husband, always said he had a good war. He had graduated from Cambridge with a degree in maths in 1935 and, when he volunteered for the RAF, almost immediately got a commission. After service in Africa, he had enjoyed, as a very young man, the responsibility of being second in command of signals in Italy.

We were one of the fortunate families: none of us was imprisoned by the Japanese, an experience from which many of the survivors never recovered. But Robert's brother, in the RAMC, was 'Lost, believed dead' in Burma and Norman's brother, a pilot in the RAF, was killed on a training exercise.

On demobilisation from the armed services the survivors were all given post-war credits, an outfit of civilian clothes and representation in the Victory Parade. Other than a nice letter from the Queen, girls in the WLA shared with the Bevin Boys the distinction of receiving none of these. The civilian clothes were no great loss. Norman had looked very handsome in his RNVR uniform; I was deeply disappointed when he came to Leeds, to announce our engagement and meet my family, wearing his ill-fitting demob suit. To be excluded from the Victory Parade was bitter. The pretext for this treatment was that none of us had been conscripted into the WLA, but neither had thousands of those who served in the armed forces. There was no excuse for the treatment of the Bevin Boys; they had all been conscripted to work down the mines. It was many years later when, for the first time, I went down a working mine, that I realised what that meant. Lady Denman, one of the founders of the WLA in 1917 and its re-creator and director from 1939 to 1945 resigned to protest against the insulting way in which we were treated.

It was the twenty first century before we were invited to lay a wreath at the Cenotaph on Remembrance Day. In 2008, we were given the medal denied us in 1945 and had our contribution to the war effort commemorated by a sculpture commissioned by the Scottish Farmers' Union.

What did I take with me from the Land Army? Certainly a voracious appetite and a strong body which has stood me in good stead for over seventy years. I started the celebration of my ninetieth birthday on the back of a half-bred Clydesdale and, with the help of Nordic sticks, can still enjoy the Pentland Hills. My love of animals, the country and Scotland were deepened and, far more important, I learnt to value people for themselves, irrespective of their background or education. From my parents, devout and practising Christians, I had known in theory about poverty and the squalor of back-to-back housing in an industrial city. During his first year at Cambridge my brother had joined the Labour Party and came home armed with Victor Gollanz's left-wing publications. My mother was a Conservative and my father a Liberal but I had followed in my brother's footsteps, I was in the Land Army before I observed the poverty of skilled and hard-working labourers and experienced the reality of being an employee. Orders had to be obeyed unquestioningly and on most farms there was no possibility of promotion to management or, without capital, to become a farmer. Sandy, the dairyman at Townhead, was exceptional. From the time they left school he and his wife must have worked from five in the morning till six at night, seven days a week and all the year round. They were in their thirties before they had saved enough money to rent the dairy at Townhead.

Jack provided the cows, the byre, the grazing and all the equipment; Sandy got the milk. By the end of the War they were able to rent a small, hilly and very run-down farm, its fields rapidly reverting to nature under a flourishing cover of gorse, bracken and ragwort. Knowing Sandy and his wife, I was sure they would turn it into a productive farm but, when I worked for them for a few weeks in 1947, there was still a long way to go.

Poverty for a seventeen-year-old living in the comfort of a farmhouse was unimportant. For the men and their families it was serious. The night I spent in the home of one of them is unforgettable. As a low paid ploughman Sandy was medically insured but his family was not. When his five-year-old daughter developed meningitis she was nursed at home by her parents. I offered to sit by her cot one night so that they might get a better night's sleep and I then experienced for the first time the reality of living conditions in a cottage considered appropriate for a farm labourer. It was stone floored and without water or electricity, the children slept in the bedroom and the parents in the only other room. This had to serve as kitchen and living room and was furnished with a bed, table, a chest of drawers, several upright wooden chairs and one rag rug. It was completely lacking in comfort.

The child survived. I had grown up in a world of private doctors, nurses and nursing homes. Babies were born and minor operations carried out at home and the arrival of the monthly nurse signalled for me the imminent arrival of yet another sibling. At Townhead I discovered the reality of medical care for the unprivileged before the National Health Service was created. The implementation of the Beveridge

Report and the provision of free or subsidised education for everybody made the Attlee years, politically, the happiest of my life. The only time I fell out with Agnes, the farmer's wife, was during the 1945 election when it became clear to her that I was not going to vote Conservative. For a week she scarcely spoke to me.

The Medal

A Benevolent Fund for Land Girls had been set up early in the war. In 1948, to my amazement, I received a cheque for £5 as a contribution to my trousseau. I had thought that the Fund was for girls in trouble! The next 60 years were not without troubles but it was 2008 before the Land Army again played a significant role in my life. Of the 80,000 girls who had served in the WLA there were 2,000 survivors to receive the medal denied us in 1945. Elaine Edwards, a Senior Curator in the National Museum of Rural Life at East Kilbride, decided to write about the 8,500 who had worked in Scotland. Her excellent book *Scotland's Land Girls: Breeches, Bombers and Backaches* is based on our memories. Expecting to find hundreds of photos to illustrate it, she discovered that most of us had been too poor to possess cameras or develop photos.

After the opening of the exhibition in the National War Museum at Edinburgh Castle both May and I, the specimen Lumber Jill and Land Girl, enjoyed the interviews that followed, if not the posing for close-up photos. More distant views were kinder: the kindest for me were those which included a tractor. In 2010, the Post Office issued stamps under

the title 'Britain Alone' to commemorate the contribution to
the war effort of those who were not in the armed forces. In
a series of eight, a photo of an unidentified Land Girl driving
a tractor was second only to Churchill reviewing a company
of the Home Guard. I was asked to take her place, sitting
on the seat of an elderly tractor at the National Museum of
Rural Life. The resulting photos were released to the Press a
few days before the general election. The timing was perfect.
Tired of pre-election politics, every paper in Scotland
published the photos, accompanied by appropriate articles. I
am now the only member of my family to have appeared in
The Sun, though not on page three.

For the last thirty-five years I have been a writer and a
freelance lecturer, so talking about the Land Army has been
easy. In most audiences there have been few people who
were alive during the war; even fewer who had any concept
of the realities of life for farm workers seventy years ago.
My own renewed interest in the Land Army has also been
a learning process, leading to research into the experiences
of other girls and return visits to Littleton and Townhead;
now amalgamated and farmed by Agnes and Jack's younger
daughter, Elizabeth Dodds and her family. Where there
had been fewer than one hundred cows there are now over
nine hundred, many of whom rarely enjoy the freedom
of the fields. But in the vast byre they did not seem to be
stressed and, ecologically, the Dodds' farming is impressive.
Vegetable gardens, once the province of the farmer's wife,
have been replaced by sun rooms and landscaped gardens.
The Townhead stable, once the social centre of the farm, is in
ruins. Inevitable but sad. Elizabeth couldn't have been more

welcoming and the son of Andy, the shepherd, has inherited his father's work as well as his wonderful smile.

A sculpture to commemorate the work of the Timber Corps was erected by the Forestry Commission in 2007. When Prince Charles, the Duke of Rothesay, unveiled the sculpture which had been commissioned by the Farmers' Union to commemorate our contribution to the war effort in 2011, there were only 14 survivors fit and able to attend the ceremony on the Crown Estate near Fochabers. Its emphasis on the 'jolly' side of work in the gangs convinced me that it was time to paint a fuller picture of the reality of life as a Land Girl.

What we had helped to achieve was impressive. Imports of timber had been reduced from 90% to 23% and 500,000 acres of land had been brought back into the fullest possible production of essential food. Britain had not starved and the Holocaust had convinced remaining doubters that the War had been justified. Perhaps Land Girls were uniquely fortunate in that their work was purely creative; for those in the armed services it had been destructive. However hard the conditions and heavy and monotonous our work could be it had only one purpose: to create food. Farming is intrinsically a rewarding occupation. I have never regretted my years in the Land Army though I wish they had been three, not five. I wish too that I had thanked my father for making me concentrate on winning the war.

Acknowledgements

I would like to thank Iseabail Macleod, for encouragement and support, as well as meticulous editing; Elaine Edwards, for help in locating material; and my granddaughter Shian Holt, for help with the mysteries of computers. I would like to thank the following for permission to use illustrations: the Dodds Armstrong family; Gill Clarke (from The Women's Land Arm: A Portrait); Jeanette Reid (from Women Warriors of Word War 2); Peter Jolly.

List of Illustrations:

1. The toughening process – author photo
2. Land Army recruitment poster – Imperial War Museum
3. The first casualty in war – author photo
4. Bondagers – Scottish Ethnological Archive
5. Bondagers - Scottish Ethnological Archive
6. Farm Labouring – the ideal – Crown Copyright
7. The Reality – Illustrated
8. Hay raking – Crown Copyright

9.   Hoeing by Randolph Schwabe – Imperial War Museum
10. Tractors – Scottish Ethnological Archive
11. Littleton – author photo
12. Jack and Agnes – author photo
13. On a horse – author photo
14. Coos on the beach – author photo
15. Map – Crown copyright
16. Kirkubright – author collection
17. Jessie King's signature – author collection
18. Tea party – author photo
19. Doris – author photo
20. Bobby – author photo
21. Jan – author photo
22. Norman – author photo
23. Mona on the Cobbler – author photo
24. Exhibition at Edinburgh Castle – author photo
25. Timber Gills – Crown Copyright
26. Bedtime by Evelyn Dunbar – Imperial War Museum
27. May and Mona – author photo
28. Certificate – author collection
29. Land Army statue with Prince Charles – Peter Jolly, Northpix
30. Government recognition from Gordon Brown – author collection